A CONEY ISLAND
of the MIND

to K.

A

CONEY ISLAND

of the

MIND

Poems by LAWRENCE
FERLINGHETTI

A NEW DIRECTIONS BOOK

EIGHTEENTH PRINTING

Some of the poems in this book have been published
in the following magazines to which grateful
acknowledgment for permission to reprint is here
given: *The Evergreen Review, Ark II - Moby I,
The Nation, New Directions 16, Chicago Review.*
Parts of the poem "Autobiography" have appeared
in *Jam Session: An Anthology of Jazz,* edited by
Ralph J. Gleason and published by G. P. Putnam's Sons.

Manufactured in the United States of America
Design and typography by Freda Browne

New Directions Books are published for
James Laughlin by New Directions Publishing Corporation,
333 Sixth Avenue, New York 10014.

CONTENTS

CONTENTS

1
A CONEY ISLAND
of the MIND

The title of this book is taken from Henry Miller's
INTO THE NIGHT LIFE. It is used out of context
but expresses the way I felt about these poems when
I wrote them – as if they were, taken together, a
kind of Coney Island of the mind, a kind of circus of
the soul.

1

In Goya's greatest scenes we seem to see
                              the people of the world
          exactly at the moment when
              they first attained the title of
                              'suffering humanity'
          They writhe upon the page
                      in a veritable rage
                              of adversity
          Heaped up
                  groaning with babies and bayonets
                              under cement skies
          in an abstract landscape of blasted trees
          bent statues bats wings and beaks
              slippery gibbets
          cadavers and carnivorous cocks
          and all the final hollering monsters
              of the
                      'imagination of disaster'
          they are so bloody real
                          it is as if they really still existed

          And they do

          Only the landscape is changed

They still are ranged along the roads
          plagued by legionaires
                              false windmills and demented roosters

They are the same people
                      only further from home
          on freeways fifty lanes wide
                  on a concrete continent
                          spaced with bland billboards
                  illustrating imbecile illusions of happiness

The scene shows fewer tumbrils
                    but more maimed citizens
                              in painted cars
          and they have strange license plates
       and engines
                    that devour America

2

Sailing thru the straits of Demos
    we saw symbolic birds
                    shrieking over us
  while eager eagles hovered
           and elephants in bathtubs
 floated past us out to sea
                strumming bent mandolins
and bailing for old glory with their ears
             while patriotic maidens
  wearing paper poppies
          and eating bonbons
  ran along the shores
          wailing after us
and while we lashed ourselves to masts
         and stopt our ears with chewing gum
 dying donkeys on high hills
         sang low songs
  and gay cows flew away
           chanting Athenian anthems
as their pods turned to tulips
         and heliocopters from Helios
     flew over us
        dropping free railway tickets
  from Lost Angeles to Heaven
         and promising Free Elections

So that
we set up mast and sail
on that swart ship once more
and so set forth once more
forth upon the gobbly sea
loaded with liberated vestal virgins
and discus throwers reading Walden
but
shortly after reaching
the strange suburban shores
of that great American
demi-democracy
looked at each other
with a mild surprise
silent upon a peak
in Darien

3

The poet's eye obscenely seeing
sees the surface of the round world
                with its drunk rooftops
                and wooden oiseaux on clotheslines
                and its clay males and females
                with hot legs and rosebud breasts
                in rollaway beds
and its trees full of mysteries
and its Sunday parks and speechless statues
and its America
                with its ghost towns and empty Ellis Islands
and its surrealist landscape of
                                mindless prairies
                                supermarket suburbs
                                steamheated cemeteries
                                cinerama holy days
                                and protesting cathedrals
a kissproof world of plastic toiletseats tampax and taxis
                drugged store cowboys and las vegas virgins
                disowned indians and cinemad matrons
                unroman senators and conscientious non-objectors
and all the other fatal shorn-up fragments
of the immigrant's dream come too true
                and mislaid
                        among the sunbathers

4

In a surrealist year
                    of sandwichmen and sunbathers
                            dead sunflowers and live telephones
        house-broken politicos with party whips
        performed as usual
        in the rings of their sawdust circuses
        where tumblers and human cannonballs
                            filled the air like cries
                when some cool clown
                        pressed an inedible mushroom button
        and an inaudible Sunday bomb
                            fell down
catching the president at his prayers
                            on the 19th green

        O it was a spring
                        of fur leaves and cobalt flowers
        when cadillacs fell thru the trees like rain
                drowning the meadows with madness
while out of every imitation cloud
                        dropped myriad wingless crowds
                            of nutless nagasaki survivors

        And lost teacups
        full of our ashes
        floated by

5.

Sometime during eternity
                some guys show up
and one of them
        who shows up real late
                is a kind of carpenter
    from some square-type place
                like Galilee
    and he starts wailing
              and claiming he is hep
     to who made heaven
             and earth
                and that the cat
       who really laid it on us
             is his Dad

And moreover
   he adds
       It's all writ down
              on some scroll-type parchments
   which some henchmen
            leave lying around the Dead Sea somewheres
      a long time ago
           and which you won't even find
for a coupla thousand years or so
             or at least for
nineteen hundred and fortyseven
            of them
      to be exact
         and even then
  nobody really believes them
          or me
           for that matter

You're hot
     they tell him

And they cool him

They stretch him on the Tree to cool

And everybody after that
                              is always making models
                  of this Tree
                              . with Him hung up
and always crooning His name
                              and calling Him to come down
                  and sit in
                              on their combo
            as if he is the king cat
                              who's got to blow
      or they can't quite make it

      Only he don't come down
                              from His Tree

Him just hang there
                  on His Tree
                              looking real Petered out
                  and real cool
                              and also
            according to a roundup
                              of late world news
      from the usual unreliable sources
                              real dead

6

They were putting up the statue
of Saint Francis
in front of the church
of Saint Francis
in the city of San Francisco
in a little side street
just off the Avenue
where no birds sang
and the sun was coming up on time
in its usual fashion
and just beginning to shine
on the statue of Saint Francis
where no birds sang

And a lot of old Italians
were standing all around
in the little side street
just off the Avenue
watching the wily workers
who were hoisting up the statue
with a chain and a crane
and other implements
And a lot of young reporters
in button-down clothes
were taking down the words
of one young priest
who was propping up the statue
with all his arguments

And all the while
while no birds sang
any Saint Francis Passion
and while the lookers kept looking
up at Saint Francis
with his arms outstretched
to the birds which weren't there

a very tall and very purely naked
                              young virgin
    with very long and very straight
                         straw hair
      and wearing only a very small
                           bird's nest
        in a very existential place
                       kept passing thru the crowd
                                  all the while
               and up and down the steps
                              in front of Saint Francis
        her eyes downcast all the while
                            and singing to herself

7

What could she say to the fantastic foolybear
and what could she say to brother
and what could she say
                        to the cat with future feet
and what could she say to mother
after that time that she lay lush
                        among the lolly flowers
        on that hot riverbank
                where ferns fell away in the broken air
                        of the breath of her lover
    and birds went mad
                        and threw themselves from trees
    to taste still hot upon the ground
                        the spilled sperm seed

8

In Golden Gate Park that day
                            a man and his wife were coming along
            thru the enormous meadow
                            which was the meadow of the world
He was wearing green suspenders
                            and carrying an old beat-up flute
                                            in one hand
        while his wife had a bunch of grapes
                            which she kept handing out
                                            individually
                        to various squirrels
                                            as if each
                            were a little joke

And then the two of them came on
                            thru the enormous meadow
which was the meadow of the world
                            and then
            at a very still spot where the trees dreamed
            and seemed to have been waiting thru all time
                                            for them
            they sat down together on the grass
                            without looking at each other
            and ate oranges
                            without looking at each other
                                        and put the peels
            in a basket which they seemed
                            to have brought for that purpose
            without looking at each other

And then
            he took his shirt and undershirt off
        but kept his hat on
                            sideways
                            and without saying anything
            fell asleep under it
                            And his wife just sat there looking
at the birds which flew about
        calling to each other

                in the stilly air
        as if they were questioning existence
                        or trying to recall something forgotten

But then finally
            she too lay down flat
                            and just lay there looking up
                                        at nothing
            yet fingering the old flute
                            which nobody played
            and finally looking over
                        at him
        without any particular expression
                        except a certain awful look
            of terrible depression

9

See
    it was like this when
                    we waltz into this place
a couple of Papish cats
                    is doing an Aztec two-step
And I says
            Dad let's cut
but then this dame
                comes up behind me see
                        and says
            You and me could really exist
Wow I says
            Only the next day
            she has bad teeth
                    and really hates
                                poetry

10

I have not lain with beauty all my life
    telling over to myself
                its most rife charms

I have not lain with beauty all my life
              and lied with it as well
     telling over to myself
         how beauty never dies
    but lies apart
       among the aborigines
             of art
     and far above the battlefields
             of love

It is above all that
        oh yes
It sits upon the choicest of
        Church seats
up there where art directors meet
to choose the things for immortality
            And they have lain with beauty
     all their lives
       And they have fed on honeydew
and drunk the wines of Paradise
          so that they know exactly how
   a thing of beauty is a joy
    forever and forever
        and how it never never
     quite can fade
        into a money-losing nothingness

Oh no I have not lain
                    on Beauty Rests like this
    afraid to rise at night
                       for fear that I might somehow miss
some movement beauty might have made

    Yet I have slept with beauty
                       in my own weird way
and I have made a hungry scene or two
                          with beauty in my bed
   and so spilled out another poem or two
     and so spilled out another poem or two
                      upon the Bosch-like world

11

The wounded wilderness of Morris Graves
    is not the same wild west
               the white man found
It is a land that Buddha came upon
              from a different direction
    It is a wild white nest
        in the true mad north
               of introspection
     where 'falcons of the inner eye'
             dive and die
      glimpsing in their dying fall
          all life's memory
             of existence
     and with grave chalk wing
           draw upon the leaded sky
  a thousand threaded images
          of flight

It is the night that is their 'native habitat'
  these 'spirit birds' with bled white wings
    these droves of plover
        bearded eagles
          blind birds singing
            in glass fields
  these moonmad swans and ecstatic ganders
              trapped egrets
        charcoal owls
            trotting turtle symbols
  these pink fish among mountains
         shrikes seeking to nest
     whitebone drones
        mating in air
    among hallucinary moons

And a masked bird fishing
                      in a golden stream
      and an ibis feeding
                      'on its own breast'

          and a stray Connemara Pooka
                              (life size)

And then those blown mute birds
                        bearing fish and paper messages
      between two streams
                  which are the twin streams
                                    of oblivion
          wherein the imagination
                        turning upon itself
          with white electric vision
                        refinds itself still mad
                  and unfed
                        among the hebrides

12

'One of those paintings that would not die'
    its warring image
                once conceived
      would not leave
              the leaded ground
  no matter how many times
                 he hounded it
                     into oblivion
Painting over it did no good
    It kept on coming through
                the wood and canvas
  and as it came it cried at him
              a terrible bedtime song
    wherein each bed a grave
             mined with unearthly alarmclocks
       hollered horribly
           for lovers and sleepers

13

Not like Dante

    discovering a <u>commedia</u>

        upon the slopes of heaven

I would paint a different kind

    of Paradiso

in which the people would be naked

    as they always are

        in scenes like that

because it is supposed to be

        a painting of their souls

but there would be no anxious angels telling them

how heaven is

    the perfect picture of

        a monarchy

and there would be no fires burning

in the hellish holes below

in which I might have stepped

nor any altars in the sky except

        fountains of imagination

14

Don't let that horse
                    eat that violin

    cried Chagall's mother

                        But he
                kept right on
                        painting

And became famous

And kept on painting
                    The Horse With Violin In Mouth

And when he finally finished it
he jumped up upon the horse
                        and rode away
            waving the violin

And then with a low bow gave it
to the first naked nude he ran across

And there were no strings
                        attached

15

Constantly risking absurdity
                     and death
       whenever he performs
              above the heads
                  of his audience
  the poet like an acrobat
          climbs on rime
             to a high wire of his own making
and balancing on eyebeams
          above a sea of faces
     paces his way
         to the other side of day
   performing entrechats
          and sleight-of-foot tricks
 and other high theatrics
         and all without mistaking
      any thing
         for what it may not be

For he's the super realist
           who must perforce perceive
      taut truth
        before the taking of each stance or step
 in his supposed advance
         toward that still higher perch
where Beauty stands and waits
        with gravity
          to start her death-defying leap

And he
     a little charleychaplin man
          who may or may not catch
   her fair eternal form
        spreadeagled in the empty air
    of existence

16

Kafka's Castle stands above the world
like a last bastille
of the Mystery of Existence
Its blind approaches baffle us
Steep paths
plunge nowhere from it
Roads radiate into air
like the labyrinth wires
of a telephone central
thru which all calls are
infinitely untraceable
Up there
it is heavenly weather
Souls dance undressed
together
and like loiterers
on the fringes of a fair
we ogle the unobtainable
imagined mystery
Yet away around on the far side
like the stage door of a circus tent
is a wide wide vent in the battlements
where even elephants
waltz thru

17

This life is not a circus where
the shy performing dogs of love
                              look on
as time flicks out
                    its tricky whip
                              to race us thru our paces
Yet gay parading floats drift by
                    decorated with gorgeous gussies in silk tights
                    and attended by moithering monkeys
                              make-believe monks
                              horny hiawathas
                    and baboons astride tame tigers
                         with ladies inside
          while googly horns make merrygoround music
     and pantomimic pierrots castrate disaster
          with strange sad laughter
     and gory gorillas toss tender maidens heavenward
     while cakewalkers and carnie hustlers
          all gassed to the gills
                    strike playbill poses
          and stagger after every
                              wheeling thing
     While still around the ring
                    lope the misshapen camels of lust
and all us Emmett Kelly clowns
                    always making up imaginary scenes
with all our masks for faces
                    even eat fake Last Suppers
                              at collapsible tables
          and mocking cross ourselves
                              in sawdust crosses

And yet gobble up at last
                    to shrive our circus souls
          the also imaginary
                    wafers of grace

18

Frightened
                    by the sound of my own voice
        and by the sound of birds
                    singing on hot wires
    in sunday sleep I see myself
                    slaying sundry sinners and turkeys
loud dogs with sharp dead dugs
                    and black knights in iron suits
        with Brooks labels
                    and Yale locks upon the pants
Yes
    and with penis erectus for spear
                    I slay all old ladies
        making them young again
with a touch of my sweet swaying sword
        retrouving them their maiden
            hoods and heads
                    ah yes
                    in flattering falsehoods of sleep

        we come we conquer all
                    but all the while
real standard time ticks on
                    and new bottled babies with real teeth
    devour our fantastic
            fictioned future

19

In woods where many rivers run
                              among the unbent hills
      and fields of our childhood
                              where ricks and rainbows mix in memory
although our 'fields' were streets
                         I see again those myriad mornings rise
      when every living thing
                              cast its shadow in eternity
         and all day long the light
                              like early morning
         with its sharp shadows shadowing
                                          a paradise
            that I had hardly dreamed of
                              nor hardly knew to think
            of this unshaved today
                              with its derisive rooks
         that rise above dry trees
                              and caw and cry
   and question every other
                         spring and thing

20

The pennycandystore beyond the El
is where I first
              fell in love
                        with unreality
Jellybeans glowed in the semi-gloom
of that september afternoon
A cat upon the counter moved among
                        the licorice sticks
              and tootsie rolls
     and Oh Boy Gum

Outside the leaves were falling as they died

A wind had blown away the sun

A girl ran in
Her hair was rainy
Her breasts were breathless in the little room

Outside the leaves were falling
                        and they cried
                        Too soon! too soon!

21

She loved to look at flowers
smell fruit
And the leaves had the look of loving

But halfass drunken sailors
staggered thru her sleep
scattering semen
over the virgin landscape

At a certain age
her heart put about
searching the lost shores

And heard the green birds singing
from the other side of silence

22

Johnny Nolan has a patch on his ass

Kids chase him
                      thru screendoor summers

Thru the back streets
                      of all my memories

Somewhere a man laments
                      upon a violin

A doorstep baby cries
                      and cries again
              like
                  a
                      ball
                            bounced
                                down steps

Which helps the afternoon arise again
to a moment of remembered hysteria

Johnny Nolan has a patch on his ass

Kids chase him

23

The Widder Fogliani
                otherwise known as Bella Donna
                    the Italian lady
                            of American distraction
the Widder Fogliani
                    was a merryoldsoul
            she had whiskers
                        on her soul
                            and her soul was a pussy
But she had a hard coming of it
                        that time I beat her
            at her own game
        which was painting moustaches
                            on statues
                        in the Borghese gardens
                    at three in the morning
and nobody the wiser
                if ever she gave
        some stray Cellini
                    a free Christmas goose

24

We squat upon the beach of love
    among Picasso mandolins struck full of sand
       and buried catspaws that know no sphinx
      and picnic papers
          dead crabs' claws
           and starfish prints

We squat upon the beach of love
      among the beached mermaids
          with their bawling babies and bald husbands
         and homemade wooden animals
            with icecream spoons for feet
              which cannot walk or love
                 except to eat

We squat upon the brink of love
   and are secure as only squatters are
     among the puddled leavings
                of salt sex's tides
       and the sweet semen rivulets
           and limp buried peckers
    in the sand's soft flesh

And still we laugh
   and still we run
     and still we throw ourselves
           upon love's boats
    but it is deeper
          and much later
              than we think
     and all goes down
        and all our lovebuoys fail us

And we drink and drown

25

Cast up

      the heart flops over

            gasping 'Love'

   a foolish fish which tries to draw

   its breath from flesh of air

And no one there to hear its death

           among the sad bushes

   where the world rushes by

           in a blather of asphalt and delay

26

That 'sensual phosphorescence
                        my youth delighted in'

now lies almost behind me
                    like a land of dreams
            wherein an angel
                        of hot sleep
        dances like a diva
                    in strange veils
            thru which desire
                        looks and cries

And still she dances
                dances still

    and still she comes
                    at me
                        with breathing breasts
        and secret lips

                and (ah)

                    bright eyes

27

Peacocks walked

under the night trees

in the lost moon
light

when I went out

looking for love

that night

A ring dove cooed in a cove

A cloche tolled twice

once for the birth

and once for the death

of love
that night

28

Dove sta amore

Where lies love

Dove sta amore

Here lies love

The ring dove love

In lyrical delight

Hear love's hillsong

Love's true willsong

Love's low plainsong

Too sweet painsong

In passages of night

Dove sta amore

Here lies love

The ring dove love

Dove sta amore

Here lies love

29

And that's the way it always is and that's the way
it always ends and the fire and the rose are one
and always the same scene and always the same
subject right from the beginning like in the Bible
or The Sun Also Rises which begins Robert Cohn
was middleweight boxing champion of his class
but later we lost our balls and there we go again
there we are again there's the same old theme
and scene again with all the citizens and all
the characters all working up to it right from
the first and it looks like all they ever think of
is doing It and it doesn't matter much with who
half the time but the other half it matters more
than anything O the sweet love fevers yes and
there's always complications like maybe she has
no eyes for him or him no eyes for her or her no
eyes for her or him no eyes for him or something
or other stands in the way like his mother or
her father or someone like that but they go right
on trying to get it all the time like in Shakespeare
or The Waste Land or Proust remembering his Things
Past or wherever And there they all are struggling
toward each other or after each other like those
marble maidens on that Grecian Urn or on any market
street or merrygoround around and around they go

all hunting love and half the hungry time not even
knowing just what is really eating them like Robin
walking in her Nightwood streets although it isn't
quite as simple as all that as if all she really
needed was a good fivecent cigar oh no and those
who have not hunted will not recognize the hunting
poise and then the hawks that hover where the
heart is hid and the hungry horses crying and
the stone angels and heaven and hell and Yerma
with her blind breasts under her dress and then
Christopher Columbus sailing off in search and
Rudolph Valentino and Juliet and Romeo and John
Barrymore and Anna Livia and Abie's Irish Rose
and so Goodnight Sweet Prince all over again
with everyone and everybody laughing and crying
along wherever night and day winter and summer
spring and tomorrow like Anna Karenin lost in
the snow and the cry of hunters in a great wood
and the soldiers coming and Freud and Ulysses
always on their hungry travels after the same
hot grail like King Arthur and his nighttime knights
and everybody wondering where and how it will all
end like in the movies or in some nightmaze novel
yes as in a nightmaze Yes I said Yes I will and he
called me his Andalusian rose and I said Yes my
heart was going like mad and that's the way Ulysses
ends as everything always ends when that hunting
cock of flesh at last cries out and has his glory
moment God and then comes tumbling down the sound

of axes in the wood and the trees falling and down
it goes the sweet cock's sword so wilting in the
fair flesh fields away alone at last and loved
and lost and found upon a riverbank along a
riverrun right where it all began and so begins again

2

ORAL MESSAGES

These seven poems were conceived specifically for jazz
accompaniment and as such should be considered as
spontaneously spoken "oral messages" rather than as
poems written for the printed page. As a result of
continued experimental reading with jazz, they are
still in a state of change. "Autobiography" and
"Junkman's Obbligato" are available on the Fantasy
LP recording No. 7002, "Poetry Readings in the
Cellar," which I made with Kenneth Rexroth and
the Cellar Jazz Quintet of San Francisco.

I AM WAITING

I am waiting for my case to come up
and I am waiting
for a rebirth of wonder
and I am waiting for someone
to really discover America
and wail
and I am waiting
for the discovery
of a new symbolic western frontier
and I am waiting
for the American Eagle
to really spread its wings
and straighten up and fly right
and I am waiting
for the Age of Anxiety
to drop dead
and I am waiting
for the war to be fought
which will make the world safe
for anarchy
and I am waiting
for the final withering away
of all governments
and I am perpetually awaiting
a rebirth of wonder

I am waiting for the Second Coming
and I am waiting
for a religious revival
to sweep thru the state of Arizona
and I am waiting
for the Grapes of Wrath to be stored
and I am waiting
for them to prove
that God is really American
and I am seriously waiting
for Billy Graham and Elvis Presley
to exchange roles seriously

and I am waiting
to see God on television
piped onto church altars
if only they can find
the right channel
to tune in on
and I am waiting
for the Last Supper to be served again
with a strange new appetizer
and I am perpetually awaiting
a rebirth of wonder

I am waiting for my number to be called
and I am waiting
for the living end
and I am waiting
for dad to come home
his pockets full
of irradiated silver dollars
and I am waiting
for the atomic tests to end
and I am waiting happily
for things to get much worse
before they improve
and I am waiting
for the Salvation Army to take over
and I am waiting
for the human crowd
to wander off a cliff somewhere
clutching its atomic umbrella
and I am waiting
for Ike to act
and I am waiting
for the meek to be blessed
and inherit the earth
without taxes
and I am waiting
for forests and animals
to reclaim the earth as theirs
and I am waiting
for a way to be devised
to destroy all nationalisms
without killing anybody

and I am waiting
for linnets and planets to fall like rain
and I am waiting for lovers and weepers
to lie down together again
in a new rebirth of wonder

I am waiting for the Great Divide to be crossed
and I am anxiously waiting
for the secret of eternal life to be discovered
by an obscure general practitioner
and save me forever from certain death
and I am waiting
for life to begin
and I am waiting
for the storms of life
to be over
and I am waiting
to set sail for happiness
and I am waiting
for a reconstructed Mayflower
to reach America
with its picture story and tv rights
sold in advance to the natives
and I am waiting
for the lost music to sound again
in the Lost Continent
in a new rebirth of wonder

I am waiting for the day
that maketh all things clear
and I am waiting
for Ole Man River
to just stop rolling along
past the country club
and I am waiting
for the deepest South
to just stop Reconstructing itself
in its own image
and I am waiting
for a sweet desegregated chariot
to swing low
and carry me back to Ole Virginie
and I am waiting
for Ole Virginie to discover

just why Darkies are born
and I am waiting
for God to lookout
from Lookout Mountain
and see the Ode to the Confederate Dead
as a real farce
and I am awaiting retribution
for what America did
to Tom Sawyer
and I am perpetually awaiting
a rebirth of wonder

I am waiting for Tom Swift to grow up
and I am waiting
for the American Boy
to take off Beauty's clothes
and get on top of her
and I am waiting
for Alice in Wonderland
to retransmit to me
her total dream of innocence
and I am waiting
for Childe Roland to come
to the final darkest tower
and I am waiting
for Aphrodite
to grow live arms
at a final disarmament conference
in a new rebirth of wonder

I am waiting
to get some intimations
of immortality
by recollecting my early childhood
and I am waiting
for the green mornings to come again
youth's dumb green fields come back again
and I am waiting
for some strains of unpremeditated art
to shake my typewriter
and I am waiting to write
the great indelible poem

and I am waiting
for the last long careless rapture
and I am perpetually waiting
for the fleeing lovers on the Grecian Urn
to catch each other up at last
and embrace
and I am awaiting
perpetually and forever
a renaissance of wonder

JUNKMAN'S OBBLIGATO

Let's go
Come on
Let's go
Empty out our pockets
and disappear.
Missing all our appointments
and turning up unshaven
years later
old cigarette papers
stuck to our pants
leaves in our hair.
Let us not
worry about the payments
anymore.
Let them come
and take it away
whatever it was
we were paying for.
And us with it.

Let us arise and go now
to where dogs do it
Over the Hill
where they keep the earthquakes
behind the city dumps
lost among gasmains and garbage.
Let us see the City Dumps
for what they are.
My country tears of thee.
Let us disappear
in automobile graveyards
and reappear years later
picking rags and newspapers
drying our drawers
on garbage fires
patches on our ass.
Do not bother
to say goodbye
to anyone.
Your missus will not miss us.

Let's go
smelling of sterno
where the benches are filled
with discarded Bowling Green statues
in the interior dark night
of the flowery bowery
our eyes watery
with the contemplation
of empty bottles of muscatel.
Let us recite from broken bibles
on streetcorners
Follow dogs on docks
Speak wild songs
Throw stones
Say anything
Blink at the sun and scratch
and stumble into silence
Diddle in doorways
Know whores thirdhand
after everyone else is finished
Stagger befuddled into East River sunsets
Sleep in phone booths
Puke in pawnshops
wailing for a winter overcoat.

Let us arise and go now
under the city
where ashcans roll
and reappear in putrid clothes
as the uncrowned underground kings
of subway men's rooms.
Let us feed the pigeons
at the City Hall
urging them to do their duty
in the Mayor's office.
Hurry up please it's time.
The end is coming.
Flash floods
Disasters in the sun
Dogs unleashed
Sister in the street
her brassiere backwards.

Let us arise and go now
into the interior dark night
of the soul's still bowery
and find ourselves anew
where subways stall and wait
under the River.
Cross over
into full puzzlement.
South Ferry will not run forever.
They are cutting out the Bay ferries
but it is still not too late
to get lost in Oakland.
Washington has not yet toppled
from his horse.
There is still time to goose him
and go
leaving our income tax form behind
and our waterproof wristwatch with it
staggering blind after alleycats
under Brooklyn's Bridge
blown statues in baggy pants
our tincan cries and garbage voices
trailing.
Junk for sale!

Let's cut out let's go
into the real interior of the country
where hockshops reign
mere unblind anarchy upon us.
The end is here
but golf goes on at Burning Tree.
It's raining it's pouring
The Ole Man is snoring.
Another flood is coming
though not the kind you think.
There is still time to sink
and think.
I wish to descend in society.
I wish to make like free.
Swing low sweet chariot.
Let us not wait for the cadillacs
to carry us triumphant
into the interior
waving at the natives

like roman senators in the provinces
wearing poet's laurels
on lighted brows.
Let us not wait for the write-up
on page one
of The New York Times Book Review
images of insane success
smiling from the photo.
By the time they print your picture
in Life Magazine
you will have become a negative anyway
a print with a glossy finish.
They will have come and gotten you
to be famous
and you still will not be free.
Goodbye I'm going.
I'm selling everything
and giving away the rest
to the Good Will Industries.
It will be dark out there
with the Salvation Army Band.
And the mind its own illumination.
Goodbye I'm walking out on the whole scene.
Close down the joint.
The system is all loused up.
Rome was never like this.
I'm tired of waiting for Godot.
I am going where turtles win
I am going
where conmen puke and die
Down the sad esplanades
of the official world.
Junk for sale!
My country tears of thee.

Let us go then you and I
leaving our neckties behind on lampposts
Take up the full beard
of walking anarchy
looking like Walt Whitman
a homemade bomb in the pocket.
I wish to descend in the social scale.
High society is low society.
I am a social climber

climbing downward
And the descent is difficult.
The Upper Middle Class Ideal
is for the birds
but the birds have no use for it
having their own kind of pecking order
based upon birdsong.
Pigeons on the grass alas.

Let us arise and go now
to the Isle of Manisfree.
Let loose the hogs of peace.
Hurry up please it's time.
Let us arise and go now
into the interior
of Foster's Cafeteria.
So long Emily Post.
So long
Lowell Thomas.
Goodbye Broadway.
Goodbye Herald Square.
Turn it off.
Confound the system.
Cancel all our leases.
Lose the War
without killing anybody.
Let horses scream
and ladies run
to flushless powderrooms.
The end has just begun.
I want to announce it.
Run don't walk
to the nearest exit.
The real earthquake is coming.
I can feel the building shake.
I am the refined type.
I cannot stand it.
I am going
where asses lie down
with customs collectors who call themselves
literary critics.
My tool is dusty.
My body hung up too long
in strange suspenders.

Get me a bright bandana
for a jockstrap.
Turn loose and we'll be off
where sports cars collapse
and the world begins again.
Hurry up please it's time.
It's time and a half
and there's the rub.
The thinkpad makes homeboys of us all.
Let us cut out
into stray eternity.
Somewhere the fields are full of larks.
Somewhere the land is swinging.
My country 'tis of thee
I'm singing.

Let us arise and go now
to the Isle of Manisfree
and live the true blue simple life
of wisdom and wonderment
where all things grow
straight up
aslant and singing
in the yellow sun
poppies out of cowpods
thinking angels out of turds.
I must arise and go now
to the Isle of Manisfree
way up behind the broken words
and woods of Arcady.

AUTOBIOGRAPHY

I am leading a quiet life
in Mike's Place every day
watching the champs
of the Dante Billiard Parlor
and the French pinball addicts.
I am leading a quiet life
on lower East Broadway.
I am an American.
I was an American boy.
I read the American Boy Magazine
and became a boy scout
in the suburbs.
I thought I was Tom Sawyer
catching crayfish in the Bronx River
and imagining the Mississippi.
I had a baseball mit
and an American Flyer bike.
I delivered the Woman's Home Companion
at five in the afternoon
or the Herald Trib
at five in the morning.
I still can hear the paper thump
on lost porches.
I had an unhappy childhood.
I saw Lindberg land.
I looked homeward
and saw no angel.
I got caught stealing pencils
from the Five and Ten Cent Store
the same month I made Eagle Scout.
I chopped trees for the CCC
and sat on them.
I landed in Normandy
in a rowboat that turned over.
I have seen the educated armies
on the beach at Dover.
I have seen Egyptian pilots in purple clouds
shopkeepers rolling up their blinds
at midday
potato salad and dandelions
at anarchist picnics.

I am reading 'Lorna Doone'
and a life of John Most
terror of the industrialist
a bomb on his desk at all times.
I have seen the garbagemen parade
in the Columbus Day Parade
behind the glib
farting trumpeters.
I have not been out to the Cloisters
in a long time
nor to the Tuileries
but I still keep thinking
of going.
I have seen the garbagemen parade
when it was snowing.
I have eaten hotdogs in ballparks.
I have heard the Gettysburg Address
and the Ginsberg Address.
I like it here
and I won't go back
where I came from.
I too have ridden boxcars boxcars boxcars.
I have travelled among unknown men.
I have been in Asia
with Noah in the Ark.
I was in India
when Rome was built.
I have been in the Manger
with an Ass.
I have seen the Eternal Distributor
from a White Hill
in South San Francisco
and the Laughing Woman at Loona Park
outside the Fun House
in a great rainstorm
still laughing.
I have heard the sound of revelry
by night.
I have wandered lonely
as a crowd.
I am leading a quiet life
outside of Mike's Place every day
watching the world walk by
in its curious shoes.

I once started out
to walk around the world
but ended up in Brooklyn.
That Bridge was too much for me.
I have engaged in silence
exile and cunning.
I flew too near the sun
and my wax wings fell off.
I am looking for my Old Man
whom I never knew.
I am looking for the Lost Leader
with whom I flew.
Young men should be explorers.
Home is where one starts from.
But Mother never told me
there'd be scenes like this.
Womb-weary
I rest
I have travelled.
I have seen goof city.
I have seen the mass mess.
I have heard Kid Ory cry.
I have heard a trombone preach.
I have heard Debussy
strained thru a sheet.
I have slept in a hundred islands
where books were trees.
I have heard the birds
that sound like bells.
I have worn grey flannel trousers
and walked upon the beach of hell.
ᵀ have dwelt in a hundred cities
where trees were books.
What subways what taxis what cafes!
What women with blind breasts
limbs lost among skyscrapers!
I have seen the statues of heroes
at carrefours.
Danton weeping at a metro entrance
Columbus in Barcelona
pointing Westward up the Ramblas
toward the American Express
Lincoln in his stony chair
And a great Stone Face

in North Dakota.
I know that Columbus
did not invent America.
I have heard a hundred housebroken Ezra Pounds.
They should all be freed.
It is long since I was a herdsman.
I am leading a quiet life
in Mike's Place every day
reading the Classified columns.
I have read the Reader's Digest
from cover to cover
and noted the close identification
of the United States and the Promised Land
where every coin is marked
In God We Trust
but the dollar bills do not have it
being gods unto themselves.
I read the Want Ads daily
looking for a stone a leaf
an unfound door.
I hear America singing
in the Yellow Pages.
One could never tell
the soul has its rages.
I read the papers every day
and hear humanity amiss
in the sad plethora of print.
I see where Walden Pond has been drained
to make an amusement park.
I see they're making Melville
eat his whale.
I see another war is coming
but I won't be there to fight it.
I have read the writing
on the outhouse wall.
I helped Kilroy write it.
I marched up Fifth Avenue
blowing on a bugle in a tight platoon
but hurried back to the Casbah
looking for my dog.
I see a similarity
between dogs and me.
Dogs are the true observers
walking up and down the world

thru the Molloy country.
I have walked down alleys
too narrow for Chryslers.
I have seen a hundred horseless milkwagons
in a vacant lot in Astoria.
Ben Shahn never painted them
but they're there
askew in Astoria.
I have heard the junkman's obbligato.
I have ridden superhighways
and believed the billboard's promises
Crossed the Jersey Flats
and seen the Cities of the Plain
And wallowed in the wilds of Westchester
with its roving bands of natives
in stationwagons.
I have seen them.
I am the man.
I was there.
I suffered
somewhat.
I am an American.
I have a passport.
I did not suffer in public.
And I'm too young to die.
I am a selfmade man.
And I have plans for the future.
I am in line
for a top job.
I may be moving on
to Detroit.
I am only temporarily
a tie salesman.
I am a good Joe.
I am an open book
to my boss.
I am a complete mystery
to my closest friends.
I am leading a quiet life
in Mike's Place every day
contemplating my navel.
I am a part
of the body's long madness.
I have wandered in various nightwoods.

I have leaned in drunken doorways.
I have written wild stories
without punctuation.
I am the man.
I was there.
I suffered
somewhat.
I have sat in an uneasy chair.
I am a tear of the sun.
I am a hill
where poets run.
I invented the alphabet
after watching the flight of cranes
who made letters with their legs.
I am a lake upon a plain.
I am a word
in a tree.
I am a hill of poetry.
I am a raid
on the inarticulate.
I have dreamt
that all my teeth fell out
but my tongue lived
to tell the tale.
For I am a still
of poetry.
I am a bank of song.
I am a playerpiano
in an abandoned casino
on a seaside esplanade
in a dense fog
still playing.
I see a similarity
between the Laughing Woman
and myself.
I have heard the sound of summer
in the rain.
I have seen girls on boardwalks
have complicated sensations.
I understand their hesitations.
I am a gatherer of fruit.
I have seen how kisses
cause euphoria.
I have risked enchantment.

I have seen the Virgin
in an appletree at Chartres
And Saint Joan burn
at the Bella Union.
I have seen giraffes in junglejims
their necks like love
wound around the iron circumstances
of the world.
I have seen the Venus Aphrodite
armless in her drafty corridor.
I have heard a siren sing
at One Fifth Avenue.
I have seen the White Goddess dancing
in the Rue des Beaux Arts
on the Fourteenth of July
and the Beautiful Dame Without Mercy
picking her nose in Chumley's.
She did not speak English.
She had yellow hair
and a hoarse voice
and no bird sang.
I am leading a quiet life
in Mike's Place every day
watching the pocket pool players
making the minestrone scene
wolfing the macaronis
and I have read somewhere
the Meaning of Existence
yet have forgotten
just exactly where.
But I am the man
And I'll be there.
And I may cause the lips
of those who are asleep
to speak.
And I may make my notebooks
into sheaves of grass.
And I may write my own
eponymous epitaph
instructing the horsemen
to pass.

DOG

The dog trots freely in the street
and sees reality
and the things he sees
are bigger than himself
and the things he sees
are his reality
Drunks in doorways
Moons on trees
The dog trots freely thru the street
and the things he sees
are smaller than himself
Fish on newsprint
Ants in holes
Chickens in Chinatown windows
their heads a block away
The dog trots freely in the street
and the things he smells
smell something like himself
The dog trots freely in the street
past puddles and babies
cats and cigars
poolrooms and policemen
He doesn't hate cops
He merely has no use for them
and he goes past them
and past the dead cows hung up whole
in front of the San Francisco Meat Market
He would rather eat a tender cow
than a tough policeman
though either might do
And he goes past the Romeo Ravioli Factory
and past Coit's Tower
and past Congressman Doyle
He's afraid of Coit's Tower
but he's not afraid of Congressman Doyle
although what he hears is very discouraging
very depressing
very absurd
to a sad young dog like himself
to a serious dog like himself

But he has his own free world to live in
His own fleas to eat
He will not be muzzled
Congressman Doyle is just another
fire hydrant
to him
The dog trots freely in the street
and has his own dog's life to live
and to think about
and to reflect upon
touching and tasting and testing everything
investigating everything
without benefit of perjury
a real realist
with a real tale to tell
and a real tail to tell it with
a real live
          barking
              democratic dog
engaged in real
             free enterprise
with something to say
             about ontology
something to say
          about reality
              and how to see it
                  and how to hear it
with his head cocked sideways
              at streetcorners
as if he is just about to have
            his picture taken
                for Victor Records
          listening for
              His Master's Voice
       and looking
           like a living questionmark
              into the
              great gramaphone
             of puzzling existence
with its wondrous hollow horn
        which always seems
      just about to spout forth
             some Victorious answer
            to everything

CHRIST CLIMBED DOWN

Christ climbed down
from His bare Tree
this year
and ran away to where
there were no rootless Christmas trees
hung with candycanes and breakable stars

Christ climbed down
from His bare Tree
this year
and ran away to where
there were no gilded Christmas trees
and no tinsel Christmas trees
and no tinfoil Christmas trees
and no pink plastic Christmas trees
and no gold Christmas trees
and no black Christmas trees
and no powderblue Christmas trees
hung with electric candles
and encircled by tin electric trains
and clever cornball relatives

Christ climbed down
from His bare Tree
this year
and ran away to where
no intrepid Bible salesmen
covered the territory
in two-tone cadillacs
and where no Sears Roebuck creches
complete with plastic babe in manger
arrived by parcel post
the babe by special delivery
and where no televised Wise Men
praised the Lord Calvert Whiskey

Christ climbed down
from His bare Tree
this year
and ran away to where
no fat handshaking stranger

in a red flannel suit
and a fake white beard
went around passing himself off
as some sort of North Pole saint
crossing the desert to Bethlehem
Pennsylvania
in a Volkswagon sled
drawn by rollicking Adirondack reindeer
with German names
and bearing sacks of Humble Gifts
from Saks Fifth Avenue
for everybody's imagined Christ child

Christ climbed down
from His bare Tree
this year
and ran away to where
no Bing Crosby carollers
groaned of a tight Christmas
and where no Radio City angels
iceskated wingless
thru a winter wonderland
into a jinglebell heaven
daily at 8:30
with Midnight Mass matinees

Christ climbed down
from His bare Tree
this year
and softly stole away into
some anonymous Mary's womb again
where in the darkest night
of everybody's anonymous soul
He awaits again
an unimaginable
and impossibly
Immaculate Reconception
the very craziest
of Second Comings

THE LONG STREET

The long street
which is the street of the world
passes around the world
filled with all the people of the world
not to mention all the voices
of all the people
that ever existed
Lovers and weepers
virgins and sleepers
spaghetti salesmen and sandwichmen
milkmen and orators
boneless bankers
brittle housewives
sheathed in nylon snobberies
deserts of advertising men
herds of high school fillies
crowds of collegians
all talking and talking
and walking around
or hanging out windows
to see what's doing
out in the world
where everything happens
sooner or later
if it happens at all
And the long street
which is the longest street
in all the world
but which isn't as long
as it seems
passes on
thru all the cities and all the scenes
down every alley
up every boulevard
thru every crossroads
thru red lights and green lights
cities in sunlight
continents in rain
hungry Hong Kongs
untillable Tuscaloosas
Oaklands of the soul

Dublins of the imagination
And the long street
rolls on around
like an enormous choochoo train
chugging around the world
with its bawling passengers
and babies and picnic baskets
and cats and dogs
and all of them wondering
just who is up
in the cab ahead
driving the train
if anybody
the train which runs around the world
like a world going round
all of them wondering
just what is up
if anything
and some of them leaning out
and peering ahead
and trying to catch
a look at the driver
in his one-eye cab
trying to see him
to glimpse his face
to catch his eye
as they whirl around a bend
but they never do
although once in a while
it looks as if
they're going to
And the street goes rocking on
the train goes bowling on
with its windows reaching up
its windows the windows
of all the buildings
in all the streets of the world
bowling along
thru the light of the world
thru the night of the world
with lanterns at crossings
lost lights flashing
crowds at carnivals
nightwood circuses

whorehouses and parliaments
forgotten fountains
cellar doors and unfound doors
figures in lamplight
pale idols dancing
as the world rocks on
But now we come
to the lonely part of the street
the part of the street
that goes around
the lonely part of the world
And this is not the place
that you change trains
for the Brighton Beach Express
This is not the place
that you do anything
This is the part of the world
where nothing's doing
where no one's doing
anything
where nobody's anywhere
nobody nowhere
except yourself
not even a mirror
to make you two
not a soul
except your own
maybe
and even that
not there
maybe
or not yours
maybe
because you're what's called
dead
you've reached your station

Descend

MEET MISS SUBWAYS

Meet Miss Subways
of 1957
See Miss Subways
of 1957
riding the Times Square Shuttle
back and forth
at four in the morning

Meet Miss Subways
of 1957
with fiftycentsize cotton plugs
in her flat black nose
shuttling back and forth
on the Times Square Shuttle
at four in the morning
and hanging on
to heaven's iron rings
with cut-up golden arms
a black weed in a black hand

You can meet Miss Subways
You can see Miss Subways
of 1957
wearing sad slacks
and matching handbag
and cruising thru the cars
and hanging on
with beat black arms
a black butt in a black hand

And the iron cars
shunting on forever
into death and darkness

o lost Ubangi

staggering thru
the 'successive ogives' of Hell
down Dante's final
fire escape

3
Poems from
PICTURES OF THE GONE WORLD
(1955)

This group of poems has been selected
from my first book, "Pictures of the Gone World,"
published in 1955 in the Pocket Series
(City Lights Books, San Francisco 11).

1

Away above a harborful
                              of caulkless houses
among the charley noble chimneypots
                              of a rooftop rigged with clotheslines
        a woman pastes up sails
                              upon the wind
  hanging out her morning sheets
                              with wooden pins
                    O lovely mammal
                              her nearly naked teats
            throw taut shadows
                              when she stretches up
to hang at last the last of her
                              so white washed sins
          but it is wetly amorous
                              and winds itself about her
            clinging to her skin
                              So caught with arms upraised
      she tosses back her head
                              in voiceless laughter
  and in choiceless gesture then
                              shakes out gold hair

while in the reachless seascape spaces

                              between the blown white shrouds

    stand out the bright steamers

                              to kingdom come

2

Just as I used to say
                love comes harder to the aged
because they've been running
                on the same old rails too long
  and then when the sly switch comes along
                                they miss the turn
    and burn up the wrong rail while
                the gay caboose goes flying
      and the steamengine driver don't recognize
                                them new electric horns
and the aged run out on the rusty spur
                        which ends up in
                the dead grass where
  the rusty tincans and bedsprings and old razor
                blades and moldy mattresses
                                lie
      and the rail breaks off dead
                        right there
      though the ties go on awhile
                        and the aged
say to themselves
                Well
                this must be the place
                we were supposed to lie down

  And they do

                while the bright saloon careens along away
    on a high
        hilltop
                its windows full of bluesky and lovers
      with flowers
                their long hair streaming
                        and all of them laughing
            and waving and
                        whispering to each other
      and looking out and
                wondering what that graveyard
      where the rails end
                        is

3

In hintertime Praxiteles
                              laid about him with a golden maul
         striking into stone
                              his alabaster ideals
uttering all
              the sculptor's lexicon
                                in visible syllables
         He cast bronze trees
                                petrified a chameleon on one
         made stone doves
                              fly
                                His calipers measured bridges
                and lovers
                              and certain other superhumans whom
         he caught upon their dusty way
                                         to death

         They never reached it then

                                       You still can almost see
                       their breath
                                Their stone eyes staring
         thru three thousand years
                                allay our fears of aging

         although Praxiteles himself
                                at twenty-eight lay dead

              for sculpture isn't for
                                   young men
            as Constantin Brancusi
                                at a later hour
                       said

4

In Paris in a loud dark winter

        when the sun was something in Provence

when I came upon the poetry

        of Rene' Char

I saw Vaucluse again

        in a summer of sauterelles

its fountains full of petals

        and its river thrown down

through all the burnt places

        of that almond world

and the fields full of silence

        though the crickets sang

with their legs

        And in the poet's plangent dream I saw

no Lorelei upon the Rhone

        nor angels debarked at Marseilles

but couples going nude into the sad water

        in the profound lasciviousness of spring

in an algebra of lyricism

        which I am still deciphering

5

Sarolla's women in their picture hats
stretched upon his canvas beaches
                              beguiled the Spanish
                      Impressionists

                              And were they fraudulent pictures
of the world
            the way the light played on them
                                    creating illusions
      of love?

            I cannot help but think
                              that their 'reality'
was almost as real as
                  my memory of today

            when the last sun hung on the hills
            and I heard the day falling
            like the gulls that fell
            almost to land

            while the last picnickers lay
                        and loved in the blowing yellow broom
resisted and resisting
                  tearing themselves apart

                                    again

                                    again

            until the last hot hung climax
which could at last no longer be resisted
                        made them moan

            And night's trees stood up

6

'Truth is not the secret of a few'
                                        yet
you would maybe think so
                        the way some
            librarians
    and cultural ambassadors and
                        especially museum directors
                                                act

        you'd think they had a corner
                                        on it
            the way they
                        walk around shaking
        their high heads and
                        looking as if they never
            went to the bath
                    room or anything

        But I wouldn't blame them
    if I were you
                They say the Spiritual is best conceived
    in abstract terms
                    and then too
        walking around in museums always makes me
                want to
                        'sit down'
            I always feel so
                            constipated
        in those
                    high altitudes

7

Fortune
has its cookies to give out

which is a good thing

since it's been a long time since

that summer in Brooklyn
when they closed off the street
one hot day
and the

FIREMEN

turned on their hoses

and all the kids ran out in it

in the middle of the street

and there were

maybe a couple dozen of us

out there
with the water squirting up
to the

sky

and all over
us
there was maybe only six of us
kids altogether
running around in our
barefeet and birthday
suits
and I remember Molly but then

the firemen stopped squirting their hoses
all of a sudden and went
back in
their firehouse
and
started playing pinochle again
just as if nothing
had ever
happened
while I remember Molly
looked at me and

ran in

because I guess really we were the only ones there

8

It was a face which darkness could kill
                              in an instant
   a face as easily hurt
                    by laughter or light

   'We think differently at night'
                         she told me once
lying back languidly

                    And she would quote Cocteau

'I feel there is an angel in me' she'd say
                         'whom I am constantly shocking'

   Then she would smile and look away
         light a cigarette for me
                              sigh and rise
and stretch
         her sweet anatomy

                    let fall a stocking

9

funny fantasies are never so real as oldstyle romances
where the hero has a heroine who has
long black braids and lets
                  nobody
kiss her ever
        and everybody's trying all the time to
run away with her
        and the hero is always drawing his
(sic) sword and
      tilting at ginmills and
            forever telling her he
loves her and has only honorable intentions and
honorable mentions
      and no one ever beats him at
            anything
but then finally one day
      she who has always been so timid
offs with her glove and says
      (though not in so many big words)
Let's lie down somewheres

         baby

10

Terrible

       a horse at night

   standing hitched alone

        in the still street

     and whinnying

       as if some sad nude astride him

had gripped hot legs on him

        and sung

          a sweet high hungry

     single syllable

11

The world is a beautiful place
                                    to be born into
if you don't mind happiness
                            not always being
                                            so very much fun
        if you don't mind a touch of hell
                            now and then
            just when everything is fine
                                    because even in heaven
                    they don't sing
                            all the time

        The world is a beautiful place
                                    to be born into
if you don't mind some people dying
                                    all the time
                or maybe only starving
                                    some of the time
            which isn't half so bad
                                if it isn't you

    Oh the world is a beautiful place
                                    to be born into
            if you don't much mind
                            a few dead minds
                in the higher places
                                or a bomb or two
                    now and then
                                in your upturned faces
        or such other improprieties
                                    as our Name Brand society
                    is prey to
                            with its men of distinction
            and its men of extinction
                                and its priests
                and other patrolmen

                              and its various segregations
        and congressional investigations
                                  and other constipations
            that our fool flesh
                        is heir to

    Yes the world is the best place of all
                                  for a lot of such things as
            making the fun scene
                            and making the love scene
and making the sad scene
                        and singing low songs and having inspirations
        and walking around
                        looking at everything
                                    and smelling flowers
        and goosing statues
                        and even thinking
                                and kissing people and
        making babies and wearing pants
                                and waving hats and
                        dancing
                                and going swimming in rivers
                    on picnics
                        in the middle of the summer
        and just generally
                        'living it up'

    Yes
        but then right in the middle of it
                            comes the smiling

                    mortician

12

Reading Yeats I do not think
                                of Ireland
but of midsummer New York
                              and of myself back then
            reading that copy I found
                         on the Thirdavenue El

        the El
                with its flyhung fans
      and its signs reading
                  SPITTING IS FORBIDDEN

        the El
                careening thru its thirdstory world
      with its thirdstory people
                  in their thirdstory doors
    looking as if they had never heard
                         of the ground

       an old dame
                   watering her plant
     or a joker in a straw
          putting a stickpin in his peppermint tie
and looking just like he had nowhere to go
                       but coneyisland

     or an undershirted guy
                    rocking in his rocker
watching the El pass by
          as if he expected it to be different
     each time

Reading Yeats I do not think
                              of Arcady
and of its woods which Yeats thought dead
                              I think instead
          of all the gone faces
                    getting off at midtown places
     with their hats and their jobs
          and of that lost book I had
                    with its blue cover and its white inside
where a pencilhand had written
                              HORSEMAN, PASS BY!

13

sweet and various the woodlark

who sings at the unbought gate

and yet how many

        wild beasts
           how many mad
in the civil thickets

        Hölderlin
           in his stone tower
or in that kind carpenter's house
        at Tübingen

        or then Rimbaud
          his 'nightmare and logic'
    a sophism of madness

But we have our own more recent
        who also fatally assumed
that some direct connection
      does exist between
    language and reality
        word and world

    which is a laugh
      if you ask me

I too have drunk and seen
      the spider

INDEX OF TITLES AND FIRST LINES

DATE DUE		

DATE DUE	BORROWER'S NAME

INDEX OF TITLES AND FIRST LINES